SMART MOVES

for Managing Your Money

Authored by
Eric Tashlein, CFP®

Edited by
Steve Higgins

Smart Moves for Managing Your Money

Authored by Eric Tashlein, CFP®
Edited by Steve Higgins

Copyright © 2012 Eric Tashlein, CFP®
All rights reserved.

ISBN: 1-4783-9185-5
ISBN-13: 9781478391852

SMART MOVES

for Managing Your Money

Authored by
Eric Tashlein, CFP®

Edited by
Steve Higgins

Contents

Introduction

1. Financial Planning

Five Steps to Creating a Financial Plan 3
Case Study in Financial Success 5
A Financial Tale 7
Stay Calm Amid Market Turmoil 9
The Recession Decade—Protect Against Stagnation 11
Protect Your Loved Ones with Insurance 15
Protecting Your Paycheck with Disability Insurance 17
Long-Term Care Insurance Can Protect Your Assets 21
A Cautionary Tale—Investing in Your Company's Stock . . . 23
Know What You're Giving up with Every Choice 25
Four Strategies to Battle Inflation 27
Adding Emerging Markets to Your Portfolio 29
Tame Volatility with Dollar Cost Averaging 31
Controlling Your Health Care Costs 33
Keeping Your Portfolio Alignment in Check 35
Windfalls Require Planning 37
Financial Advice for the Under-Thirty Set 39

2. Retirement Planning

Manage Your Retirement Savings Plan 43
Seven Common Retirement Planning Mistakes 47
Five Steps to Make Your Money Last. 51
When You Near Retirement 53
Take Retirement Advice from Ben Franklin. 55
How Retirees Can Combat Low Interest Rates 59
Five Tips On Paying Off Your Mortgage 61
Pros and Cons of Roth IRA Conversions 63
How to Handle Your IRA Rollover. 67
When You Lose Your Spouse 69
Happiness Is A Positive Cash Flow 73
Stay Healthy for a Happy Retirement 75
Living Abroad in Retirement 77

3. Special Topics

Raising Financially Savvy Kids 81
Buying Your Dream Car 83
Getting the Right Price for Your Family Business. 85
Protect Yourself against Identity Theft 89
Charitable Giving Comes in Many Forms 93
Weighing the Benefits of Renting versus Owning a Home. . .95
Inheritance Poses Challenges for Parent and Child 97
Discussing the Future with Your Elderly Parents 99
How to Find the Right Financial Planner. 101

Introduction

Financial planning is the art of managing your financial future. The goal is to help maximize your assets while reducing your level of risk.

Sound simple? It's actually a difficult undertaking, since there are many variables involved in earning money and investing it wisely. Your life situation changes, your goals evolve, and financial markets and the economy undergo continual upheaval.

As a Connecticut resident, you face particular challenges since you live in a high-income, high-tax state with high energy costs thrown in for good measure.

The good news is that sitting down to clarify your goals and create a financial plan is half the battle. The other half is finding an experienced and knowledgeable financial advisor to help you craft your plan and then skillfully implement it.

Meet Eric Tashlein. Eric is a CERTIFIED FINANCIAL PLANNER™ professional and founding principal of Connecticut Capital Management Group, LLC, located at 67 Cherry Street in Milford. He enjoys helping people manage, organize, and simplify their financial affairs.

Eric is a financial columnist for the *New Haven Register* and a contributing author to a previous financial planning book titled *Giving*. He has written articles on financial topics, has appeared on local TV shows, and has been quoted by major media outlets including *Money* magazine, *Financial Advisor*, and *USA Today*.

Eric is an active member of the financial planning community and has served as president of the New Haven Council Board of the Financial Planning Association of Connecticut. He frequently speaks about investment, retirement, and tax reduction strategies to retirees and pension/401(k) plan participants at area corporations and organizations.

Eric and his family are lifelong area residents. He is active in many different charities and organizations including Milford Rotary, the New Haven Manufacturers Association, and the Milford Hospital Foundation Board.

Connecticut Capital Management Group is a financial services firm offering advisory and wealth management platforms to high net worth individuals, business owners and executives, retirees, and "soon to be" retirees. The firm takes a comprehensive approach to financial planning and wealth management, acting as your personal chief financial officer.

Connecticut Capital Management Group's experienced financial advisors review your current and long-term financial goals and conduct a thorough analysis of your financial situation and risk tolerance. They meet with your estate planning attorney, your accountant, or other advisors, taking an integrated approach guided always by your individual needs and objectives. One of the firm's primary goals is to explain the complexities of the financial world to you in a way that is meaningful and easy to understand.

Eric believes in fostering long-term relationships built on trust. He maintains regular contact with his clients and adjusts their portfolios and financial plans as their life situation and aspirations evolve over time.

Eric has reached a high level of professional achievement as an advisor, and he also remains grounded in a common-sense view of financial planning. The articles in this book provide an enlightening and entertaining introduction to Eric's approach to helping others to protect and accumulate wealth.

Smart Moves for Managing Your Money is divided into three sections:

- **Financial Planning** includes seventeen articles on various aspects of investment management.

- **Retirement Planning** includes thirteen articles about planning for your retirement years.

- **Special Topics** includes nine articles on various topics ranging from buying your dream car to finding the right financial planner for you.

You can reach Eric Tashlein at 203-877-1520 or through www.connecticutcapital.com.

Connecticut Capital Management Group, LLC is located at 67 Cherry Street, Milford, CT 06460.

Note: All of the articles in this book originally appeared in the *New Haven Register.*

This book is for informational purposes only and should not be construed as personalized investment advice or legal/tax advice. Please consult your advisor/attorney/tax advisor. Please note that tax laws are subject to change and the articles contained in this book were current as of 2012.

Registered Representative, Securities offered through Cambridge Investment Research, Inc., a Broker/Dealer, Member FINRA/SIPC. Investment Advisor Representative, Cambridge Investment Research Advisors, Inc., a Registered Investment Advisor. Cambridge Investment Research, Inc., Connecticut Capital Management Group, LLC and Connecticut Benefits Group, LLC are not affiliated.

FINANCIAL PLANNING

Five Steps to Creating a Financial Plan

Google Earth is the ultimate toy for peering down the road to see where your journey may take you. It will show you some of the perils that lie ahead and the routes that appear safest.

Financial plans are very similar and can be far more valuable. In the hyper-fast world that we live in, take the time to set goals and peer down the road into your financial future. Your goal should be a journey that is filled with fewer "white knuckle rides"—with the ultimate goal of attaining your personal vision.

Like lawyers without wills, the majority of Americans are wishful thinkers when it comes to doing the smart planning that can turn financial dreams into reality. In the words of Thoreau, "In the long run, we hit only what we aim at."

If you spend more time planning your summer vacation than your retirement each year, that should be a wake-up call for you to enlist the services of a professional financial planner.

Here's your easy five-step checklist to get on track with a financial plan:

1. **Gather your information** such as wills, investment statements, insurance, pension information, and other important documents.

2. **Find a financial planner**. You can use financial planner association websites like www.fpanet.org, which lists planners in your area. Interview several and be sure to ask lots of questions about their experience, education, and how they are paid. This website also offers helpful checklists of questions to ask during an interview.

3. **Schedule a "financial physical"** with the planner you choose so you can assess your state of financial health.

4. **Have a written financial plan** prepared by your planner, and work with your planner to update it as you head towards retirement and beyond. Most high-end planners will identify six to seven areas that need attention during the initial interview meeting. Common areas of concern include portfolios not in alignment with goals and risk tolerance, income tax and capital gains bills that are higher than they need to be, and wills that have not been updated.

5. **Move forward with confidence**. Once your planning has been vetted, and you have your punch list to work on, you are on your way to enjoying a healthier retirement.

Once you've gotten on top of your retirement planning, you can look back with satisfaction knowing you have given yourself the best chance of succeeding with the financial means available to you.

Case Study in Financial Success

Born to a middle-class family that encouraged a strong work ethic at home and at school, Olivia graduated with honors from the University of Connecticut with a business degree and a dream to open a world-class service business. She had nothing to lose since she could live at home cheaply while she built her wedding planning business.

She sought out the best in the business, and they became her informal board of directors. Steve, the best wedding caterer in the state, encouraged her to save from an early age into a Roth IRA. Although it wasn't tax deductible, it would allow her to grow her monies tax deferred and come out tax free during retirement. He told her it was akin to paying tax on the acorn and harvesting the tree for free. She listened and saved as much as she could.

Olivia then sought the advice of a legendary wedding planner, and her vision became crystal clear. Susan, the wealthy wedding planner, encouraged her to use 'best of breed" service providers, not only in her profession, but also when choosing a CPA, attorney, and financial planner.

As she followed her carefully crafted mission statement, her business took off. Her attorney drafted documents to protect her from liability and drafted a will in the unlikely case something happened to her. Her CPA helped her improve her cash flow and reduce her taxes. Her financial planner explained the benefits of disability income protection if she couldn't work, and the power of life insurance for paying off her debts if the unthinkable occurred.

Olivia read the best business books and hired the best employees, then set up a generous 401(k) plan to retain them.

Olivia, now thirty, decided to maximize her 401(k) deferral with an eye toward retiring at fifty-five with a sizable nest egg. She could afford to save a lot since the home she chose to buy with her husband was understated but in a great neighborhood with excellent schools. The realtor and the mortgage broker had both suggested they could afford twice the house, but Olivia recognized she would need to save for their children's education.

Fast forward to age fifty-five: Olivia has enjoyed an amazing career helping people on their special day while garnering the respect of her family by being there for her children's special moments.

Financially, she will enjoy income sources from her wedding planning business that is being sold to her key employees, from the building that she purchased to house the business, and from the taxable savings she set aside that will cover her expenses until she can tap into her 401(k) and IRA savings without penalty.

Olivia is fictional, of course. Few people manage to live their lives with that level of planning, commitment, and follow through. Luck always plays a part as well. However, this tale is intended as a model—especially for young people—to see how planning ahead and making choices with the long term in mind can help you attain financial success while crafting a life of meaning and productivity.

Not one to sit still, Olivia is thinking of consulting in her field so she can keep her mind active, and she looks forward to volunteering at local charities. She has enjoyed a life well lived, and she is a financial planner's dream client.

A Financial Tale

In the early 1960s a set of identical female twins were born to a hard-working couple in Milford. The girls both ran on the same track team, achieved the same grades, enjoyed the same friends, and had crushes on the same boys at school.

Their parents set the tone early when it came to their spending and work habits. Their father worked several jobs at a nearby factory and their mother was a lunch aide in one of the local grammar schools. The dad prided himself on fixing things around the house, bought low-mileage used cars, and seemed to wear the same flannel shirts and jeans for decades at a time. Their mother ran a tight household, shopped when items were on sale, and prided herself on being involved with her children's lives while holding down a job. Having discipline, it wasn't surprising that the parents would save a good portion of their pay each week for retirement and to send the first generations of their family off to college.

When the twins graduated college at the age of twenty-one, they both began working in the same profession. On their birthday they discussed their financial goals—to retire together at age sixty-five. One decided to save $5,000 a year for the next ten years in her Roth IRA account and then stop saving completely when she turned thirty. The other bought a BMW right out of college and decided she would have a good time for now and start saving when she turned twenty-seven. She promised her sister she would then begin saving

$5,000 a year in her Roth IRA until she turned sixty-five, so they could retire together in Florida.

The financial results of this fanciful story, using a hypothetical 9 percent return and the power of compounding, would be astounding: The first sister would have set aside $50,000 over the ten-year period, and the second sister would have saved $190,000 over the 38 years spanning her 27th and 65th birthdays. When they both reached sixty-five they would have nearly amassed the same amount of money, rendering them identical twins again from a financial standpoint! Each would have amassed around $1,690,000 while taking completely different paths.

What's the moral of this hypothetical story? Start saving as early as possible and when it comes to saving enough for retirement, the most important step is committing yourself to saving money over an adequate period of time. The magic of compounding should do the rest.

Stay Calm Amid Market Turmoil

The stock market in 2011 brought back memories of roller coaster rides at Lake Compounce: unnerving turns, stomach-churning drops, and breathtaking advances. The Dow Jones Industrial Average rose and fell by one hundred or more points many more sessions than usual.

The market calmed down in early 2012, but volatility can return at any time—so investors need to be prepared for it.

Volatility can hit due to negative economic factors such as rising oil prices, high unemployment, and anemic housing markets, or positively due to improving economic data in the United States or overseas. Stock prices also can fluctuate following either tragic events or highly positive events.

As an investor, how do you decide whether to pay more attention to the negative news or the positive news? Planning for both outcomes is the smart choice. Here's how:

Stay calm. Negative headlines will always be with us. Don't let them rattle you. After all, stocks came back nearly 100 percent from the lows experienced in early 2009.

Focus on the long term. Market ups and downs become more important as you approach retirement, but unless you're pretty close to giving up that paycheck, you don't need to focus on short-term worries.

Rely on your plan. You should have a long-term financial plan firmly in place, based on your individual needs and goals. Don't change it unless your needs or goals change.

Use asset allocation, diversification, and rebalancing. Your plan should include the right mix of assets and investment strategies and should be reviewed and adjusted regularly to keep you on track.

Keep the faith. While short-term economic shocks can cause you some anxiety, remember that long-term trends continue to bode well, such as growth in emerging markets, improvements in consumer credit totals, and increasing capital spending by businesses.

The Recession Decade – Protect against Stagnation

The previous decade left many investors humbled. If you look at the Dow Jones Industrial Average from 2000 to 2009 it resembles a flat line on a heart rate monitor. The Standard & Poor's 500 and NASDAQ indexes look worse.

The economy may improve, but what if the market indexes remain flat over this decade as well? Take the following steps to safeguard your retirement savings against the possibility of another no-growth decade:

Set goals and have a plan. Assess your monthly expenditures and annual savings. Gather your Social Security income estimates and your pension and investment statements and determine how much money you will have available when you stop working. Keep in mind that things change—for instance, the Social Security system will likely be overhauled—so develop some options if you can. The old rule of thumb was to replace 70 percent of current income in retirement. However, that percentage is on the low side for many retirees after accounting for travel, hobbies, and health care expenditures.

Be tax sensitive. The fallout from the current, unprecedented government spending spree will include higher taxes. Capital gains rates will likely increase, along with income tax brackets. Look at your 1099 income over the past five years and evaluate whether your investments are tax sensitive. Are your portfolio managers employing trading tactics that incur short-term capital gains taxes? Tax drag on portfolios can substantially cut into your portfolio values, income, and net worth. If your portfolio is concentrated in a few stocks or industries, now may be a good time to reposition your holdings before capital gains rates reset. Even better, if you have investments with losses, tax loss harvesting can result in lower taxes. Finally, compare after-tax returns on your taxable bonds with the returns on tax-free bonds and consider making appropriate changes.

Review your portfolios. Portfolios often fail to take advantage of asset classes that complement each other. If we find ourselves in another volatile decade, you will want to consider balancing your portfolio into segments that allow for contingencies. For example, having several years worth of living expenses set aside in good quality short-term bond investments and cash can allow for peace of mind during stock market declines. During the 1970s, when growth was subdued and taxes were elevated, dividends became an important component of many portfolios. Owning dividend-paying stocks in a low-growth, low-interest rate environment can be helpful.

Take advantage of employer plans. Many employers offer a match for 401(k) plan contributions, and these can be effective forced savings plans. Having a portion of your pay coming automatically out of your check each week can be a blessing, and an employer match amounts to free money being deposited to your account.

Be debt sensitive. Carrying less debt allows for less stress during uncertain times. Before interest rates head up from historic lows, now may be a good time to assess your balance sheets and pay off high-cost loans. Finding yourself debt free in retirement can be liberating.

One caution: While it's important to protect yourself against continued market stagnation, make sure a significant portion of your portfolio is poised to take advantage of potential growth over the next ten years. Don't forget the first part of the expression, "Hope for the best and prepare for the worst."

Protect Your Loved Ones with Insurance

If you love someone, you should purchase a proper amount of life insurance coverage in order to provide for him or her in case something happens to you. But the old rule of thumb—buy ten times your salary – doesn't necessarily apply in an era of high mortgage debt coupled with skyrocketing college costs and low interest rates.

To avoid leaving a legacy of debt and distress, consider the following factors to determine how much life insurance you need in order to take care of your loved ones:

Determine your likely debt. Take your outstanding loans and add future costs such as college tuition, children's weddings, legal liabilities and funeral costs. A common goal is to have a policy that would pay off the house and fully fund college for your children in case you die prematurely.

Understand your Social Security survivor's benefits. Social Security will pay benefits to your survivors, meaning your widow or widower as well as your children and dependent parents, depending on their age and other factors. Keep in mind that Social Security projections can easily change in an environment of excessive government debt.

Know your family's income requirements. Life insurance can pay off your debts, and certain policies will also keep a portion of your income flowing to your survivors. For instance, if you have $300,000 of debt to retire and would like to continue providing $50,000 a year pre-tax to your family after you pass away, you will need a lump sum of $1.25 million based on a hypothetical 5 percent return, not adjusted for inflation.

Understand term vs. life policies. Once you know the amount of life insurance you need to purchase, you must decide whether to buy term life, which covers you only for a certain period of time, or whole life, which covers you for your entire lifetime. Term is simpler and cheaper. Whole life policies vary widely and offer a myriad of extra benefits, but can be expensive and confusing. Ultimately, your decision should be based on reaching the appropriate level of coverage first. If you can only afford term insurance, then by all means buy term insurance. If you can afford to buy a combination of term and one of the many types of permanent life insurance, then consider doing so. Just be wary of any sales person who wants to sell you a $500,000 whole life policy when you need $1.5 million to properly cover your family.

Look into laddering. For some people it makes sense to buy term life policies with different terms, i.e. a 10-year policy, a 20-year policy and a 30-year policy. You may have a need for substantially more coverage over the next ten years, for instance, than you will likely have for the twenty years after that period. Compare the cost of buying one 30-year policy with the cost of buying a set of policies that reduce the amount of coverage you have step by step, as in a ladder.

In the end, the most important thing is to buy some life insurance if you have a family that depends on your income, even if you can only afford one 10-year term policy. You can always add more policies in later years as your income and assets increase.

Protecting Your Paycheck with Disability Insurance

One of the foundations of a strong financial plan is addressing the need for income in the event you're disabled. According to the LIFE Foundation, one in five Americans will be disabled for at least twelve months prior to age sixty-five.

If you own a home or have monthly bills to pay, you should consider obtaining adequate disability income protection. Disability insurance providers will usually cover up to 60 percent of your employment income if you become disabled.

In an era when many Americans have little savings and are living paycheck to paycheck, this valuable coverage can act as a lifeline. If you believe the Social Security Administration will step in and save the day, think again: The federal agency denies nearly half of all disability claims it receives, and the average payment is a paltry $1,003 a month. In a high-cost state like Connecticut, that amount may only cover your property taxes and put food on your family's table.

In considering disability insurance, the primary decision is whether to buy an individual policy or purchase a group policy through your employer, assuming one is available. Keep in mind that both types of coverage can limit benefits for preexisting medical conditions. Here are some of the factors to weigh:

- Individual policies often offer stronger policy provisions, such as "own occupation" coverage that can cover you if are disabled and cannot perform the major duties of your job. Some of these policies will continue to pay even if you are able to rejoin the job force in a different career at a similar level of pay.

- You can customize individual policies by adding important riders such as inflation protection, which will increase your monthly benefits based on the Consumer Price Index.

- Individual policies often offer rate guarantees and sometimes offer provisions that will not allow the insurer to cancel your coverage once it takes effect.

- Group disability coverage can be less expensive. According to Tim Falanga, an employee benefits specialist at the Managing Agency Group in Shelton, if you own or work at a small employer, you can often obtain a reasonable group disability policy provided the company has two or more full-time employees.

- If you are a professional, you may be able to tap your professional association's plan.

- Group disability policies often limit "own occupation" coverage to two years, followed by less favorable contract language such as "any occupation" provisions, which will deem you no longer disabled if you are able to work in any job based on your education, training, or experience.

Whatever your employment circumstances, you should explore this often forgotten piece of your financial plan. After all, you insure your health, your home, your vehicles, and hopefully your life, so it only makes sense to protect your income as well.

Long-Term Care Insurance Can Protect Your Assets

Could your savings or retirement plan handle a $315,000-plus hit to the bottom line? For most, that amount would be devastating.

According to the Connecticut Office of Policy and Management, the average nursing home stay in our state will cost you $348 per day, with two-and-one-half years being the average time spent in a facility. The cost for a private room would up the ante, and these average costs do not reflect the lost wages and stress suffered by family members who are involved during this painful journey.

To add insult to injury, Medicare and your employer health plan will not usually cover long-term stays in a nursing home, adult day care site, or assisted living facility.

The choices you face are not easy: Either pay for uncovered care out of your pocket to the tune of $127,000-plus per year or consider purchasing a long-term care policy. These policies are not inexpensive, but they do offload some of the risks to an insurance company.

If you are blessed with a substantial six-figure retirement income and high net worth, you may get away with "self insuring" some or all of the costs. Otherwise we would suggest looking into a long-term care policy that fits into your budget.

As you review policies, you should note how much the policy covers each day. If the policy pays $250 per day, be sure you can handle the difference through your available sources of income or assets. Most policies have an elimination period: Coverage will not kick in until after a set period of time.

Most policy options will cap your total benefits. If your cap were $500,000, that would be the maximum benefit you would receive unless you add an inflation rider to the policy. Costs for nursing home care and assisted living are rising around 5 percent a year, so an inflation rider can protect your benefits from erosion.

Consider purchasing a policy that is part of The Connecticut Partnership for Long Term Care, because these policies offer Medicaid asset protection. In alliance with the state of Connecticut, private insurance carriers offer policies that pay for long-term care and also protect the policyholder's assets.

Partnership policies protect asset amounts equal to what your policy has paid in benefits. In other words, if you must spend down your assets to qualify for Medicaid, you will be able to retain assets equal in value to the total amount your policy pays for your care. For more information go to www.ct.gov/opm.

The state offers educational workshops on these offerings from time to time. In addition, a well-versed financial planner or long-term care insurance professional can help you sort through the myriad of choices available with these policies.

When you consider the possible cost of care, investing in a high-quality long-term care insurance policy could save you a lot of financial heartache in the long run.

A Cautionary Tale—Investing in Your Company's Stock

If you're an employee of a publicly traded company or have built up a substantial position in an individual stock, you should be aware of the devastating declines in certain "household name" stocks over the past decade—and plan accordingly.

Most recently, the 2010 Gulf of Mexico oil spill led BP retirees to lose their dividend income, which had helped many of them pay their bills. In addition, BP's stock price plunged 60 percent in the three months after the disastrous spill.

BP joins a list of many other fallen stars over the years such as Enron, GE, and Pfizer. An old adage offers sage advice: A single stock may make you rich, but it won't necessarily keep you there. Here are some ways to ensure you don't fall into this trap:

- **Follow the 5 percent rule.** Ideally, any given holding should constitute no more than 5 percent of your overall portfolio. That way, a precipitous drop in one investment won't cost you any sleep.

- **Use dollar-cost averaging, in reverse.** If you already have too many of your investment eggs in one or more big baskets, extricate yourself by using the concept of dollar-cost averaging, only in reverse: Set a pre-programmed time every quarter to sell a portion of the stock over a twelve- or twenty-four-month period, and buy other equities or fixed-income investments with the proceeds.

- **Look to your 401(k).** When you signed up for the company 401(k) plan, investing in your company's stock may have been the best option. However, it may pay to look at other options within the plan and transfer some investment funds over. It's a way to diversify in a tax-efficient manner.

- **Consider a charitable gift annuity.** If you have a really large position, you can transfer equity to a charity, and in return the charity provides a partial tax deduction and a lifetime stream of annual income. You receive income on the entire dollar amount because the charity does not have to pay any capital gains taxes.

- **Place collars and options on the holding.** Set limits below and above the current stock price. If the stock hits a limit, you automatically sell shares.

- **Detach emotionally from your company's stock.** Lots of people were loyal to Enron—and lost their life savings. Don't get caught in the same sad situation.

Know What You're Giving up with Every Choice

One of the main themes in Economics 101 is the discussion of opportunity costs. The phrase refers to the cost of pursuing one direction while forgoing the other choices that may be available.

For example, it's the price you pay at a diner for a deli sandwich, soda, and pickle five days a week versus brown bagging it. Say you typically spend $10 a day for lunch out, and the cost of making lunch for yourself is $2.50 a day. Your opportunity cost over the course of a thirty-five-year career is the difference between the two choices each day plus interest.

In this case, if you had invested the $7.50 per day difference over the span of your career it would amount to the staggering sum of $258,000 based on a 7 percent return without taking taxes into consideration. In other words, you paid a price of $258,000 in lost opportunities to invest your money.

This discussion takes on an entirely new perspective with unemployment rates near 10 percent amid a lackluster economy. If you celebrate your sixtieth birthday and suddenly get downsized by your employer, that lunch money could make the difference between paying off the mortgage and heading into bankruptcy court.

With recent polls by Rasmussen suggesting that the majority of Americans feel as if we are still in a recession, analyzing your choices makes a lot of sense. If you are trying to save for retirement and climb the economic ladder to the good life, can you live without the prestige of driving a 2010 BMW 5 series with the requisite car payment and higher insurance costs?

You have other choices. For instance, you could buy a used luxury car with extended warranties. Or you could buy a brand new Ford family sedan. Either way, the payoff is that you can invest the difference in cost for your future.

As you make choices in the midst of today's perilous economy, keep the concept of opportunity cost in mind. And remember the concept doesn't only apply to money; it applies to anything of value. An opportunity cost could be in the form of lost time, lost enjoyment, or lost learning.

When it comes to investing, the point is not to live like a pauper, forgoing a new sweater and eating macaroni and cheese every night. The point is to make sensible choices so that you can live comfortably today while building the financial foundation for a comfortable future for yourself and your family.

Four Strategies to Battle Inflation

The global economy is recovering, and that is sending demand soaring for commodities, consumer products, food, and oil. That in turns sends prices heading upward in the United States as supplies come under pressure.

Economists may say that "core inflation" (which excludes volatile food and gas prices) is stable, but all it takes is a trip to the grocery store for you to understand that your purchasing power is being affected by rising prices.

Inflation is a very basic and real threat to your retirement savings, because it eats away at the purchasing power of the dollars you are setting aside for your future. Therefore continuing inflation will force you to withdraw more money from your savings—unless you take the inflation factor into account from the beginning.

Famed investor Warren Buffett has called inflation "the ultimate tax." He said "the best investment against inflation is to improve your own earnings."

Be wary of inflation. From 1969 to 1981, inflation measured by the Consumer Price Index was nearly 8 percent on an annualized basis, according to the DFA Matrix Book. As a result, stocks in the S&P 500 index had an inflation-adjusted real return of -2 percent over that period.

One-month certificates of deposit didn't fare much better. Over the years, I have heard many folks mention how high rates for certificates of deposit (CDs) were during this period; however, adjusted for inflation their returns would have been less than 1 percent. If you add the exorbitant income taxes of the period into the equation, this would have nearly wiped out the returns achieved during the period.

With the amount of money printed during the last few years, we would recommend that you have a conversation with your advisor about the potential impact of inflation on your retirement accounts. The Federal Reserve is trying to keep inflation rates consistent and will do what it can to keep a lid on runaway inflation as we move forward. As a country, however, if we don't get our economic house in order, the Federal Reserve will have a tough battle on its hands.

Fortunately there are several strategies your advisor can help you implement to minimize the damage inflation can inflict on your retirement portfolio. There is no need to sit by idly while rising inflation ravages your retirement savings.

Adding Emerging Markets to Your Portfolio

For investors, emerging-market economies have become synonymous with long-term growth potential coupled with volatility.

The world's gross domestic product (GDP) is now evenly divided between the developed world (nations such as the United States, England, Japan and Germany) and the developing world (India, China, Brazil, Turkey, etc.), according to the Organization for Economic Cooperation and Development. The OECD predicts by 2030 the developing world will produce 60 percent of world GDP.

The International Monetary Fund predicts that GDP among emerging-market economies will grow 6.1 percent in 2012, compared with an anemic 1.9 percent in the developed world. Much of the emerging-market growth will occur in greater Asia, with India and China currently two of the leaders in an increasingly competitive field.

In 2010, China became the second largest economy on the planet, surpassing Japan—and with the United States clearly in its sights.

In 2001, economist Jim O'Neil, now chairman of Goldman Sachs Asset Management, came up with the term BRIC, which included Brazil, Russia, India and China. He later coined the term MIST, which added the next group of larger emerging-market countries, which includes Mexico, Indonesia, South Korea and Turkey. Beyond the MIST lie younger economies including parts of South America, Eastern Europe, Africa, Asia and the Middle East.

From an investor perspective, these markets allow for participation in countries with a growing working class and increasing consumerism, which boosts demand for the products and services of local companies as well as multinationals. They also allow you to benefit from commodity-driven growth in countries that export oil, natural gas, or precious metals.

The downside of these investments is that emerging-market governments can be subject to occasional upheaval, internal corruption, and human and property rights violations.

When formulating your investment mix, we advise taking a balanced approach to emerging markets. Making aggressive, overweight bets in these markets can lead to gut-wrenching changes in your monthly statements.

For those without an appetite for direct investments overseas, you can invest in domestic multinational corporations that stand to benefit from growth in the developing world. Many companies within the S&P 500 derive a growing portion of their revenues from conducting business in these markets. In addition, companies listed on U.S. stock exchanges adhere to a higher standard from a regulatory standpoint.

With this approach, you hope that a rising tide abroad translates into a raised ship on our shores.

Tame Volatility with Dollar Cost Averaging

In these volatile markets, having a large lump sum to invest can be akin to a surfboarder staring at the mother of all cresting waves. Imposing waves and volatile stock markets have kept many hidden behind the breakwaters.

For those intelligent souls not willing to invest their fortune in a lump sum and face the wrath of poor market timing, dollar cost averaging is worth considering.

Dollar cost averaging is a way to invest a sum of money in equal parts over a period of time. It is a tool to lessen the chance of making a lump sum investment during a market top. It also can work against you in a rising market.

Dollar cost averaging is well suited for skittish investors who recognize the value of investing in the markets but wish to do so by slowly wading in. In some cases we suggest a six-month schedule of regular investments, while in other cases a twelve-month schedule may be more appropriate.

Investing regular amounts over time (dollar cost averaging) may lower your average cost per share. Unfortunately, periodic investment programs cannot guarantee profit or protect against loss. This long-term strategy involves continuous investing, regardless of fluctuating price levels, and, as a result, you should consider your financial ability and risk appetite to continue to invest during periods of widely fluctuating price levels.

With dollar cost averaging, you buy a fixed dollar amount of a particular investment asset on a regular schedule, without regard to price. That way you buy more shares when the price is low and fewer shares when the price is high. As you can see, it's a way to enforce intelligent market discipline.

As the name of the technique suggests, your average cost per share will fall over time. Here's an example: Say you buy $100 worth of Company ABC every month for three months. The price is $33 a share the first month, so you obtain three shares. In the second month the average price drops to $25 a share, so you obtain four shares, and in the third month the price falls to $20, so you obtain five shares. Looking back, you bought twelve shares for about $25 a share.

That's a clear improvement over buying twelve shares the first month at $30.

Of course, if the share price had risen by $5 each month, your average cost would have risen as well, and therefore you would not have gained as much at the end of the period as you would have with a lump-sum purchase. So if you believe that equity prices are going to rise steadily over the next few years, dollar cost averaging may not be for you.

During a period of high volatility, though, dollar cost averaging can provide real protection from the shocks of an up-and-down market. It's flexible, too: We may suggest increasing or decreasing your flow of funds based on market events.

Controlling Your Health Care Costs

Along with death and taxes, annual increases in health care premiums seem inevitable. If you're like most consumers, you will raise the amount of your co-pays and deductibles to keep your premiums from hitting the stratosphere.

One way to keep a lid on rising health care costs is to consider opening a Health Savings Account. Long a mystery to health care consumers, these plans can make sense in the right situation. In essence, you are coupling a savings account with a high-deductible health insurance plan.

In theory, going with a high-deductible health plan should decrease your premiums. With the extra "savings" you can set up a tax-deductible Health Savings Account to save for out-of-pocket costs. When you incur a medical expense, you can tap the savings account to pay the bill.

Some participants with low use may find themselves with surplus savings at the end of the year, which can be reserved for future use. If your savings account grows well beyond the deductibles, you could invest a portion into a bond- or stock-based investment portfolio within the HSA.

For 2012, the maximum deductible for a single individual is $6,050 and for a family $12,100. The most you can put into an HSA in 2012 is $3,100 for an individual and $6,250 for a family.

You may be a candidate for an HSA if your worst-case scenario finds you breaking even or ahead of the game after taking into account maximum out-of-pocket costs and premium savings vs. traditional health plan options. As a bonus, certain costs like dental and eyeglasses can be paid out of your HSA. For a full list, go to www.IRS.gov. Withdrawals made for expenditures other than health care may be subject to tax and certain penalties.

Be sure to shop around when looking for an HSA. Find an agent who specializes in health care to guide you through the vast array of choices. Tim Falanga, who specializes in employee benefits at the Managing Agency Group in Shelton, suggests working with an agent who will determine if an HSA is a good fit for you and your company.

On a personal note, my family switched to an HSA years ago. Sometimes we are ahead of the game, and other years we find ourselves breaking even. Just be sure to look at the traditional options at each renewal to ensure that traditional plans aren't a better choice. For high-level consumer health care, you may find the traditional options are just as good or better depending on your circumstances.

Keeping Your Portfolio Alignment in Check

In a perfect world all of our financial chores would be automated so we could spend all of our time pursuing our passions and enjoying friends and family. However, it's important to stay on top of your finances and not let financial chores slide.

One of the areas in your financial life that requires some thought is your asset allocation mix after a market run up or downturn. The process of keeping your portfolio mix in line with your risk tolerance can be addressed by rebalancing.

For example, if your ability to sleep at night is hindered by having more than 50 percent of your investments in the stock market, you will want to rebalance your holdings in a systematic way.

Let's say your portfolio has grown from a diversified mix of 20 percent cash, 30 percent bonds, and 50 percent stock, and you are now holding 58 percent stock. You may address the shortfall in your bond and cash holdings with the following rebalancing techniques:

- Sell 8 percent of the stock holdings to bring the equity portion back in line with your risk tolerance and preferred portfolio mix. Take the proceeds and reinvest in the cash and bond holdings to get back in line with your ideal 50/50 mix. For taxable portfolios, please keep the tax consequences in mind. Hopefully, the holdings that you sell have imbedded long-term capital gains rather than short-term gains, which include assets that are sold in one year or less from date of purchase and are taxed at the highest marginal tax rate. The difference in taxation can be considerable. In any given year, you probably have a "dog" of an investment that has fallen in value. Selling this at a loss may help offset some of the taxable gains that may occur when you rebalance. Keep in mind that only short-term losses can offset gains that are short term in nature.

- Make additional investments into the asset classes that are underweighted. For example, if you are regularly adding to your portfolio, as in the case of a 401(k) plan, you could increase your investments in the areas that require additional amounts to bring your mix up to optimal levels.

- Delegate these chores to a qualified financial advisor or opt for date-based portfolios within your 401(k) plan, provided they are cost effective and have performed well. These measures can take some of the legwork out of the rebalancing process.

Once your portfolio is properly rebalanced, set regular intervals to check on your portfolio alignment. It's vital to keep your asset allocation mix properly aligned with your financial planning goals.

Windfalls Require Planning Too

If you are the beneficiary of a large liquidity event—say you sell your business, receive a large inheritance, earn a lucrative retirement package, or hit the lottery—take a tip from Rudy Giuliani's playbook on managing during a crisis: Slow down, take a deep breath, and try your best to think rationally. Hopefully you've planned for this day in advance, but if not, your first call should not be to a boat broker!

Making financial decisions abruptly can cause problems, especially when those decisions involve a significant sum of money. Your first calls should go out to your financial planner, your accountant, and an estate planning attorney. Request a joint meeting of the minds to start crafting a new financial plan based on your new circumstances. You must:

Know your situation. Prepare for the meeting by gathering your financial records and statements, estimating your cash flow needs, and compiling your most recent brokerage and insurance statements, estate plans, and tax returns.

Understand what may change. Before you take any significant action, be sure you understand how your windfall affects your income, your tax picture, your retirement options, and your estate plans. If your liquidity event involves the loss of a loved one, consider adding a therapist to your list of counselors to help you deal with your grief.

Revisit your goals. If you have not defined your personal and financial goals, now is the time to do so. If you have, a liquidity event should spur you to revisit your list and perhaps revise it in light of your new circumstances.

Be flexible. Financial planning touches on every area of your life, and each aspect of planning may affect other areas. For example, some of the discussion in your meeting may revolve around current issues such as paying off mortgage debt and college funding shortfalls, and those are issues that will affect retirement and estate planning.

Taxes are key. If your estate is large you must consider the impact on estate taxes. According to Gene Torrenti, a Hamden attorney and estate planning expert, "Now may be a great time to take advantage of 'dollar for dollar' and leveraged gifting since asset levels are still depressed from the recession. This will remove all future appreciation of the asset from the individual's estate." Combined with the specter of future government tax increases, you have added incentive to pass the financial torch to several generations of loved ones. Your accountant should prepare an estimate of tax liability.

The direction your planning takes will depend to a large extent on what type of liquidity event you experience. For instance, if your windfall comes in the form of equities or other non-cash assets, part of the discussion will involve how to best leverage those assets. A large retirement package will require tax coordination of stock option selling. But whatever the source of your newfound liquidity, careful planning will help ensure that it remains a blessing and not a curse.

Financial Advice for the Under-30 Set

They have been called Generation Y and Echo Boomers. Eighty million strong and larger than the Baby Boom generation, these young Americans were born between 1982 and 1997.

Although the exact dates of this generation have been debated, they are the torchbearers who will carry the United States into the future over the next fifty years. They will support Social Security and confront challenges from globalization to the nation's aging infrastructure.

Some have been stereotyped as flip-flop-wearing slackers, but in reality they are seeking a better work-life balance than their parents. With their superior technology skills, they just may pull it off.

As a group, they've watched their baby boomer parents overindulge and thankfully tend to be better savers than their moms and dads. They also seek home ownership and a workplace setting that imparts a genuine sense of community. On these two points, I have suggestions that have worked for Generation Xers, Boomers, and the Greatest Generation that might be considered timeless pieces of advice.

Over the years I have worked with many savvy "Millionaire Next Door" types, and their lives often leave clear clues to the secrets of their success. When they were young, they started saving early through retirement accounts, and with the power of compounding growth over decades they amassed sizable nest eggs.

The financially fittest folks had no problem buying good quality used cars and rarely used financing except when it came to buying a home or upgrading their small businesses. The homes they bought were not typically McMansions but were purchased with the thought in mind that if they ever had children they could still pay the mortgage if mom or dad stayed home with the kids.

The beauty of this thought process was that it allowed these young couples to amass significant savings while they were both working since the mortgage payment was not eating up all of their income. Even if one spouse stopped working, they could often leave their savings to grow for their later years. Once the kids were old enough, the stay-at-home parent sometimes re-entered the workforce to shore up paying for college or to boost retirement savings.

Of course, this strategy is more difficult to pull off today due to runaway property taxes and higher utility costs associated with home ownership. But if you're willing to sacrifice keeping up with the Joneses and their latest list of disposable toys and gadgets, it remains a sensible strategy to build a secure financial future.

RETIREMENT PLANNING

Manage Your Retirement Savings Plan

In the 1960s if you worked in the corporate or government sector you could count on a monthly pension, health care benefits, and a gold watch as part of your retirement package. Fast-forward to today and you will find an altered landscape.

Corporations long ago recognized that having to fund substantial obligations to a guaranteed pension plan could lead them into bankruptcy during tough financial times. That's why most companies have switched to a different model that relies on generating returns from investments fueled by contributions from both employer and employee.

For evidence the private sector did the right thing, look no further than the public sector: Local towns and state governments continued to offer traditional pension plans and are now faced with a tsunami of debt obligations during a period of declining tax revenues.

Traditional pensions are known as "defined benefit plans" while the newer models, characterized by 401(k) plans, are known as "defined contribution plans." While the transition to defined contribution plans has helped corporations stay fiscally sound, it presents employees with a challenge: Become more involved with your own retirement planning or face potentially dire consequences.

Traditional pension plans offer employees a guaranteed income after they stop working based on their salary and how many years they were members of the pension plan. With a 401(k) plan, a portion of the employee's pay goes into an individual account, with some employers contributing money to the account as well. The money is invested in the stock market based on the employee's individual choices, and it grows tax free until retirement.

Clearly the trend toward using 401(k) accounts shifts the burden for retirement savings from employers to individual employees. As an employee, you must be actively involved in managing your 401(k) account. Here are some tips:

- Join your company's 401(k) plan as soon as possible. The longer money stays invested the higher your likely returns.

- Contribute as much as you can up to the maximum allowed by the plan. The more money you invest the more you earn, and the more your taxable income is reduced.

- Keep a separate savings account for emergency expenses. If you withdraw your 401(k) money early you will pay a penalty.

- Get full matching contributions. If your company offers matching contributions, invest at least the amount necessary to obtain the full match.

- Diversify your investments. In choosing which investments your 401(k) funds will go into, set up a diversified portfolio by investing in several different types of stock funds and a bond fund or money-market fund.

- If you manage your 401(k) plan smartly you can build up a nice nest egg for your retirement years and take your future into your own hands.

Seven Common Retirement Planning Mistakes

Even investment guru Warren Buffett makes financial mistakes sometimes, but having an extra billion or two on hand helps to ease the pain. For the rest of us, making major mistakes with retirement planning can severely impact your income and lifestyle during the golden years.

The list of mistakes people make is long and too often repeated. Here are some of the errors we regularly identify:

- **Paying too much in taxes.** Capital gains and income taxes can easily decrease investment returns by more than 1 percent per year. When possible, utilize tax-efficient investments in your taxable accounts, especially if your tax bracket is over 20 percent.

- **Not taking advantage of employer plans.** Many employers will contribute a 3 percent match toward your 401(k) contribution. Take advantage of this free money whenever possible. If you earn $75,000 per year and fail to participate in a plan that offers a similar match, it would cost you $2,250 per year. If you're over age fifty, take advantage of so-called "catch-up" provisions that allow you to set aside extra money tax-deferred in your 401(k) plan.

- **Retiring with debt.** Retirement can be costly enough without having to make large mortgage and car payments. Do whatever you can to reduce or eliminate these expenses prior to retirement. For some, the only option may be selling the home and moving to a lower-cost area.

- **Buying toys without investment income to cover the cost.** Taking a page out of the "Rich Dad Poor Dad" book series, we suggest holding off on toy buying until your investment or real estate income easily covers the costs. Let's face it: We have all run into "Mr. Big" who wears a Rolex, lives in a McMansion, drives a leased convertible Mercedes, cruises on his financed yacht—yet has no net worth due to huge debt. His income barely covers his expenditures. Best quote of all time describing this guy comes from an old Texas saying: "Big Hat, No Cattle."

- **Being under-insured.** Nothing can harm your retirement years like health problems, so it's imperative to ensure you have adequate insurance coverage that includes health, disability, long-term care insurance, and life insurance.

- **Not getting advice.** Most individuals retire without previous experience as a retiree. If you make a large financial mistake preceding retirement, it may be difficult to recover. Try to find a seasoned advisor who works with pre-retirees and retirees who have similar financial needs to yours. If you are a business owner or corporate executive, find an advisor who works with other successful business owners or executives that have retired well.

- **Not creating a pre-retirement and post-retirement financial plan**. Your retirement can last many years, so it's not a stage of life that you want to take lightly. That means you need a solid financial plan leading up to it and governing your actions afterwards.

Retirement can be a challenging time of life no matter what level of success and wealth you have achieved. Do yourself a favor and make sure you are well prepared.

Five Steps to Make Your Money Last

Markets have ebbed and flowed precipitously over the past decade, causing boomers and seniors alike to have concerns about outliving their retirement assets. Falling 401(k) plan values combined with a backdrop of increased life expectancies support some of these fears.

According to the Centers for Disease Control, the average life expectancy in America is nearing seventy-eight; so planning for a thirty-year retirement is not out of the realm of possibility. Here are some thoughts on reducing the risk of running out of funds during your retirement:

Review your holdings. Many investors tend to use infomercial guru Ron Popeil's cooking strategy in their portfolio management—they "set it and forget it." In today's market, not reviewing holdings on a regular basis is a mistake.

Work longer. Being able to draw a paycheck works in your favor during difficult markets. The longer you can add to your 401(k) and hold off hitting your portfolio for income, the better off you'll be. Working longer may also provide you with additional coverage for health insurance expenses. In addition, Social Security payouts tend to increase when you delay applying for benefits.

Pay off debts. Heading into retirement with a mortgage and other loans creates undue stress and hardship. Make paying off your outstanding notes a priority as you ease into retirement. For some, downsizing or relocating may be the best solution. In addition, having a handle on your expenses is a vital part of this process.

Check your pension benefits. For those fortunate enough to have a traditional pension, you have been blessed with a means of receiving income for your life as well as your spouse's life as one of your options. Many of these plans do not offer cost-of-living adjustments, and you will need to position some of your other investments for growth. Certain annuities offer guaranteed income riders for the life of the investor and the spouse as well. The downside can be the cost of an annuity and the possibility that no money will be left for inheritance purposes.

Make hard choices. For some, the thought of reducing lifestyle in retirement is impossible, and boomers in particular are not always willing to alter their spending. For these individuals, your choice is to find ways to increase income whether through work or repositioning of assets.

When You Near Retirement

Congratulations on your pending retirement! For those about to sail off to a life of leisure or part-time work, the rise in endorphins is palpable. Visions abound of time spent with friends and loved ones traveling to warmer climates, fishing, golfing, reading, and exercising to your heart's content.

Unfortunately, many individuals make the leap having put more time into their travel plans than their financial plans. With retirement planning, you want to do it right the first time, since many of us won't get a second chance! Here is a checklist of items to handle before you leave your work obligations behind you:

- **Do a "dry run."** If you were planning to take a road trip across the United States, you would likely plan your driving routes based on your ultimate destination. Do your best to estimate your monthly costs, and then run retirement projections that combine your assets, income, and spending needs. It's a good idea to incorporate varying returns, inflation, taxes, health-care costs, and life expectancy while you're at it. A good financial planner can help in this area.

- **Update your wills.** Some of you have wills that haven't seen the light of day in decades, and others are in dire need of one. It's important to update your wishes and create trusts when necessary to reduce or eliminate undue estate taxes. Taking control of your assets in the event of your passing should be high on everyone's "to do" list.

- **Pay off your debt.** It's hard to enjoy your retirement years when large bills hit your mailbox every month. Consider if your situation warrants paying off the mortgage and other outstanding debt. We often find in initial meetings with prospective clients that they have considerable holdings in cash or equivalents. If it's determined that enough has been set aside to plan for emergencies and upcoming expenses, we will often discuss paying down debt, especially if the interest rates and tax implications warrant it.

- **Pretend you're already retired.** Over the next few months, try living as if you're retired already and see what estimates or goals you may need to adjust as you head into your next stage of life.

Once you retire, please feel free to send me a postcard!

Take Retirement Advice from Ben Franklin

Founding Father Benjamin Franklin could teach most of us a lesson or two on retirement planning. America's original entrepreneur said, "A penny saved is a penny earned," and "Beware of little expenses, a small hole can sink a great ship."

In the context of saving and spending, these quotes illustrate a difference in the mindsets of individuals who amass a healthy net worth and those who continue to struggle to pay the bills—much less put aside savings.

The fifteenth of seventeen children, Franklin did not come from a wealthy family. His father was a soap and candle-maker in Boston. He built wealth on his own through small business ventures and diligent savings. His formal schooling ended at age twelve, but he continued to educate himself via an insatiable appetite for reading and learning. A tireless worker, Franklin was able to "retire" in his early forties to pursue his vast interests. Ultimately, his writing skills and popularity abroad would help Americans secure freedom from the British.

If Franklin were alive today, I'm sure he would offer sage comments on how little we save and how much we spend. Here are a few of the things he did say on this subject:

- "By failing to prepare, you are preparing to fail."

- "An investment in knowledge pays the best interest."

- "Creditors have better memories than debtors."

- "He that is good for making excuses is seldom good for anything else."

- "He that goes a borrowing goes a sorrowing."

- "Never leave that till tomorrow which you can do today."

And yes, he really did write, "Early to bed and early to rise, makes a man healthy, wealthy, and wise."

Franklin certainly practiced what he preached. During his long life he was a well-known author and printer, politician, postmaster, scientist, and diplomat. He made discoveries in electricity and meteorology and invented the lightning rod, bifocals, a carriage odometer, the Franklin stove, and other items. He established the nation's first public lending library, and he signed both the Declaration of Independence and the U.S. Constitution.

With such an active life, Franklin became a wealthy man, and he put his money to good use by forming trusts for both Boston and Philadelphia. He gave one thousand pounds to each city (about $55,000 in today's dollars) in 1790 with instructions that the money should gather interest for two hundred years and then be spent for good causes. Each trust generated several million dollars, and the money has gone to charitable, community, and educational needs.

America's most famous self-made man preached a gospel of foresight and prudence. He counseled people to make saving money a top priority, and he also provided a superb example of using hard work to get ahead. His final act was to create an example of generosity—not to mention the power of compound interest—by donating a significant portion of his wealth to the people of the two major cities in his life.

In our time, the average personal saving rate dipped to nearly 1 percent of income in mid-2005, according to the U.S. Bureau of Economic Statistics, before rebounding to its current 6 percent rate in the face of a historic economic slowdown. Since a major reason for that slowdown has been identified as over-spending by average citizens, I can't help but wonder: If more people had absorbed the wisdom of Benjamin Franklin, could we have avoided the 2007 recession altogether?

Either way, you should understand that adopting Franklin's common-sense practices concerning money and debt could go a long way toward restoring your own fiscal health and helping you create a secure and happy retirement.

How Retirees Can Combat Low Interest Rates

Low interest rates can be a positive force for corporations and individuals with high-cost debt. However, they can be bad news for retirees who live off their interest payments.

With 10-year U.S. Treasuries hitting record lows and inflation heating up, many individuals are losing buying power, especially if income taxes are taken into consideration. According to St. Louis Federal Reserve data, if you had invested $100,000 in a 10-year Treasury note in 2001, it would have yielded approximately $5,000 per year if held to maturity. In September 2011, the same investment will yield an estimated $2,000, or 60 percent less, before taxes. That's a far cry from yields of the past.

Those with traditional pension plans that are fully funded and managed well should consider themselves blessed in this environment. For retirees without substantial pension income, the choices are more difficult.

Common sense would dictate reviewing all of your available options before considering higher risk investments. Look to your budget first to see what you can reduce. Also, since loan rates are reduced, look to see if refinancing certain debt makes sense for you.

For some, part-time work may be a viable solution. For those heading into retirement or already there, having a financial plan drawn up or a formal portfolio review can help you make smarter choices with your money.

From a portfolio perspective, your next step would be to have all of your investments thoroughly reviewed to determine what areas can be improved upon to make up for any income shortfalls.

For those willing to leave the comfort of certificates of deposit and other safe investments, choices to improve income flows will usually mean taking on higher risk or less liquid alternatives. Annuities, real estate investment trusts, dividend-paying stocks, riskier bond classes, and other alternative investments will fall into these categories.

Take time to understand how these alternatives work and make sure you have a handle on the risks and rewards available with these options. Make sure to plan for contingencies and the inevitable changes that will occur in the markets and in your life as you review potential choices.

Five Tips On Paying Off Your Mortgage

For those nearing or in retirement, the question of whether or not to pay off the mortgage usually comes to mind. Part of our collective American dream has always been home ownership followed by a mortgage-burning celebration heading into retirement. The Great Recession has altered or pushed back this goal for some, but the question still remains.

Studies by the Boston College Retirement Research Center suggest that paying off the mortgage makes sense in the majority of cases. Here is a checklist when making your decision:

- **Compare investment returns**. Let's say you have a 5 percent mortgage and receive a mortgage interest deduction that effectively reduces the interest rate to 4 percent. You now have a basis for comparison. If you are a conservative investor and expect to earn less than 4 percent on your other investments, you should consider paying off the mortgage.

- **Weigh source of funds**. The best monies to use to pay off the mortgage would be from your taxable accounts. If you have all of your money locked up in tax-deferred retirement accounts you will need to take income taxes and a potentially higher tax bracket into account. For example, if you have an outstanding mortgage of $75,000 and your withdrawal bumps you into a 30 percent overall income tax bracket, you would be faced with taking an additional $22,500 from your IRA or 401(k) plan to adjust for the tax bill. We suggest you have your financial advisor or CPA run the numbers before making a final decision.

- **Downsize away your debt**. Another strategy to effectively cancel your mortgage would be to sell your home and downsize to a cheaper home mortgage free. For some, this may entail moving to a lower-cost area.

- **Address other debt**. If you have other loans or debt that are more costly such as credit card balances, you will need to take care of those debts first.

- **An alternative**. If paying off your mortgage isn't realistic right now, you may want to consider refinancing. Mortgage rates today are at or near all-time lows, offering many homeowners a chance to bring down their interest payments. Just be sure to ask for a "good faith" estimate, which would disclose all the fees and potential charges that are part of the refinancing process.

Pros and Cons of Roth IRA Conversions

The IRS lifted the $100,000 income limit on Roth IRA conversions in 2010, so now anyone can convert their traditional IRAs and 401(k) accounts over to a Roth. Converting to a Roth can offer many benefits, but there are factors you must consider in making this decision, and even then you should meet with your tax and legal advisors before moving forward. Here are the primary issues:

Pros

- **The unique features of a Roth IRA.** The Roth IRA gives you the ability to receive tax-free income for life after you reach 59½ as long as the Roth has been in place for at least five years. Roth IRAs may be passed to beneficiaries free of income taxes. You do not have to take minimum distributions, nor would your surviving spouse. Non-spouse beneficiaries have to take minimum distributions. (Converted amounts can be distributed without penalty after five years, beginning January 1 of the year of conversion and ending December 31 of the fifth year. Each conversion has a separate five-year holding period. Distribution of earnings before completing a five-year holding period and attaining 59½ may be subject to tax and a 10 percent penalty).

- **A Roth IRA can benefit people in many different life stages.** Those who should consider converting include younger people who have time to make up for paying the taxes; anyone whose tax rate will remain high during retirement; those not planning to draw income from the Roth, and those with longer life expectancies; and anyone wishing to leave the account to their children or to non-spouse beneficiaries, especially if they are in high tax brackets.

Cons

- **Conversion from an IRA to a Roth requires paying taxes on any pre-tax contributions, plus any gains.** If you are under 59½, the money used to pay these taxes cannot come from your traditional IRA without a 10 percent penalty.

- **Annuities can present problems.** If your IRA is invested in an annuity, look carefully at the riders and a conversion's effect on them.

- **Charitable considerations.** If you plan to leave your IRA funds to charity you may be better off leaving them in a traditional IRA because the charitable bequest would be tax deductible.

- **Legislators could amend the Roth IRA taxation rules.**

- **Lost medical deductions.** Expenses for medical or long-term care services can reduce taxable income received by a traditional IRA, but not with a Roth IRA.

- **Temporary effects on income taxes and deductions.** A Roth conversion may push your income up enough so that your Social Security income becomes taxable. If you're on Medicare, a conversion may boost your Part B premiums. College financial aid or deductions may be affected.

- **Complexity may cost you.** If you have after-tax monies in your current IRA, you must prorate the taxes owed when converting. All IRA accounts must be included for this calculation. If you decide to roll your 401(k) plan into a traditional IRA later in the year, this will throw off your calculations.

- **Distribution rules.** If you are 70½ and may convert, you must take your required annual distribution first.

Converting to a Roth IRA can offer advantages, including new options for retirement planning. If you are considering a conversion, be sure to focus on your overall financial picture and your individual goals in making your decision.

How to Handle Your IRA Rollover

If you are planning to retire soon or you have lost your job, it's time to think about rolling over your 401(k) or profit-sharing plan into an Individual Retirement Account. Even if you remain employed, an IRA rollover can enable you to consolidate accounts or use investment strategies that are not available within your employer's plan, especially when it comes to estate planning.

One of the advantages of IRAs is their portability. However, rollovers can turn into a minefield because the IRS rules governing these transactions are quite complex. Here are some issues to keep in mind:

Two choices. You can either have the monies from your employer-sponsored account sent directly to an IRA you have established, which is called a Direct Rollover, or you can have the funds sent to you personally, which is called an Indirect Rollover. A Direct Rollover is the simplest way to go, because the funds remain in a tax-advantaged account.

Indirect rules. If you receive the funds personally, the IRS's "60-Day Rule" requires you to deposit the funds into an IRA within 60 days or risk paying taxes and penalties. If you are under 59½, you could pay a 10 percent penalty for early withdrawal as well. Moreover, with an Indirect Rollover your employer will withhold 20 percent of the funds for potential tax liabilities, and you will have to make up that amount when you deposit the funds into an IRA.

While you may eventually be reimbursed, failing to add the 20 percent out of your own pocket will subject you to income tax on the unfunded amount.

Time limit. You are only allowed to transact one Indirect Rollover every twelve months per IRA account. There is no limit on the number of times you can make Direct Rollovers, which are transfers from one trustee to another trustee.

Loan clean up. If you took out any loans from an employer-sponsored retirement plan, you have to pay off the outstanding balance before you roll over the funds into an IRA. Otherwise the balance amount will be treated like a distribution and become taxable.

Caution: big gains. If you have highly appreciated company stock within your employer plan, you need to do further financial planning before considering an IRA Rollover, to avoid paying more in taxes than you need to.

Beneficiary bottom line. Be sure you name a beneficiary to the IRA, because if you die without doing so your loved ones may lose a significant portion of their inheritance as the funds pass to your estate and become subject to probate rules. By the same token, be sure to update your beneficiary form if your life situation changes due to divorce, death, or other circumstances. Finally, keep copies of your beneficiary forms, as it is not uncommon to hear of custodians losing these forms and wreaking havoc on the family.

For many retirees, IRAs represent their largest retirement asset. Minor mistakes can compound into major penalties when it comes time to roll over your account. Be sure to have your advisor team on board as you make these important retirement decisions.

When You Lose Your Spouse

One of the most trying situations we face in life is the loss of a spouse. From a financial planning perspective, it can produce significant challenges for the surviving spouse, especially when the deceased played a major role in making financial decisions.

If you lose your spouse, it's important that you take charge of your financial future. After all, your spouse would not have wanted you to suffer financial difficulties on top of all the other challenges you are facing. Here are the steps you need to take:

Assess your financial status. Too often a surviving spouse is left in the dark regarding the family finances, especially when their former partner handled all of the paperwork. Your first step must be to review your finances: assess your cash position, investments, current bills and income, and investigate potential benefits from your spouse's employers such as health insurance, group life insurance, and retirement plans.

Notify and amend. Most couples jointly hold multiple accounts and contracts, and in some cases a surviving spouse must notify the organizations involved and place accounts in their name only. Contact life insurers, banks, and credit unions first. The next step is to contact credit card companies, but keep in mind that some companies may have based the terms of the card on the combined income of both spouses, so they may now reduce your credit limit. Before amending any contracts held jointly, consult with an attorney or financial advisor. Any changes could affect estate planning or other financial plans.

Get help. You may want to enlist your children or immediate family members to help you with your finances, but I would suggest you lean on your family members for emotional support and find a trusted financial planner or accountant to guide you. Of course, it's OK to enlist children and family members to assist with certain financial matters such as paying bills, but it's a good idea to have an objective party involved as well—especially when it comes to more complex issues such as investments and taxes.

Arm yourself with knowledge. Take time to educate yourself by reading about personal finance. It's vital that you understand the basics of handling money and investing in order to make the best decisions possible.

Pause and reflect. Hold off on major decisions involving investments, selling your home, or moving out of the area. Now is a good time to reassess your goals and to create or amend your financial and estate plans. Rash decisions during this vulnerable time can result in higher costs, more taxes, and painful regrets if you make poor choices due to emotional distress.

All of these suggestions relate to dealing with the loss of a spouse after it happens, but there are also steps you can and should take while you are both alive and well. To prepare for the inevitable:

Work together on financial issues. Both spouses should be involved in making decisions about personal finances, and both should play a part in carrying out those decisions. Consider establishing a relationship with a financial advisor while both spouses are healthy. That will ensure professional help is in place once the inevitable occurs.

Keep records accessible. As a couple, develop a list of where to find assets, wills, business documents, tax return information, and other financial records. Keep the list in a safe place that is easily accessible in a time of need. The list should also include contact information for financial and legal professionals.

Losing a spouse is one of life's most stressful challenges. While there is no way to alleviate the pain and sadness that accompanies this life-changing event, you can make sure it doesn't also devastate your financial future.

Happiness Is a Positive Cash Flow

When planning for your retirement, consider how many "buckets of income" you can draw from. Retirees with the healthiest cash flows have multiple sources of income.

Those with five or more buckets seem to have the best ability to handle the economic and market swings that accompany decades in retirement. In an ideal scenario, you would receive regular checks from a traditional pension, Social Security, rentals, business or employment income, portfolios, annuities, and savings accounts.

Your pension. If you are approaching retirement, now is a good time to request pension estimates from your company's human resources department. Typically, you will have a myriad of options such as a single life payout or payments during your lifetime and a reduced amount payable to your spouse in the event of your death. Work with your financial advisor to determine the best option for your situation.

Your Social Security benefits. Social Security automatically sends your monthly estimate on an annual basis. When incorporating Social Security estimates into your financial plan, keep in mind a sobering June Congressional Budget Office report that found Social Security payouts will exceed tax revenues this year. The report goes on to say that during the coming decades either benefits reduction or additional tax increases will have to occur.

Continuing to work. For those planning to work part time, such employment can be a comforting source of income during your early retirement years. The old rule of thumb considered 80 percent of pre-retirement income adequate during retirement. However, we find that the first years of experiencing "the good life" are often accompanied by escalating expenses. Trips, hobbies, and home improvement projects that were long put off tend to appear on the "to do" list, so having employment income should allow you to put a smaller dent in your savings. It will also help you ride through volatile periods in the stock market and economy that will inevitably occur.

Rental property. If you have rental property, now is a good time to assess the remaining terms on the mortgage and the potential income generation during your lifetime after accounting for maintenance, periods of vacancy, and higher taxation of the property.

Your portfolio. From a portfolio perspective, obtain a dividend estimate and formulate a comfortable spending plan that will allow the investments the opportunity to grow over your lifetime.

Other resources. Annuity payout estimates and savings assessments should complete your picture of income sources.

In the words of an old coach and successful Oregonian advisor, Thomas Gau, "Happiness is a positive cash flow." We hope good health, friends, and family also accompany you on your journey.

Stay Healthy for a Happier Retirement

An average sixty-five-year-old American couple will face $197,000 in un-reimbursed medical costs during their retirement years, according to the Center for Retirement Research at Boston College. This figure includes co-pays and uncovered medical expenses such as eyeglasses, prescriptions, and dental care.

That amount does not include nursing home costs, which would add an average $63,000 to the total. The center also states there is a 5 percent risk of exceeding $570,000 in overall un-reimbursed medical costs, a number that is out of reach for many retirees.

This study begs the question, "What are my costs if I retire in optimal health?" The center conducted another research project designed to evaluate whether being in excellent health versus poor health will save you money over your lifetime. Unfortunately, it appears that we will still be writing sizable checks to our physicians and pharmacies either way.

The second study found that good health can reduce your average medical costs per year, but over the long run your costs will actually increase due to higher longevity and a greater chance of needing nursing home care. In other words, if you stay healthy you are more likely to live longer, so naturally you will incur more medical expenses.

Please don't hang up your gym clothes just yet. There is a silver lining for people who take care of their health that goes well beyond the numbers: A recent study on emotional health and well-being finds that good health promotes happiness.

As part of the Gallup-Healthways Well-Being Index, Gallup interviewed a large group of people aged sixty to sixty-nine and found that good health produces significantly higher well-being scores. The survey studied levels of enjoyment, laughter, stress, worry, depression, perceived respect, and personal fulfillment, among other factors. Among the sixty-year-old participants, those in excellent health scored an average "89" on the Well-Being Index while those in poor health scored an average of "58."

Taking these various studies into account, it seems clear that you should make the effort to eat healthy food and exercise regularly so you have a greater chance of enjoying your golden years. Jason Leydon, owner of the CrossFit Milford gym, concurs. Jason believes that people who exercise vigorously and eat healthy, unprocessed foods tend to have higher energy levels and a lower chance of obesity-related illnesses.

What's the bottom line? Being healthy and happy is a better way to go through retirement, even if you will need to generate more income to account for a longer life.

Living Abroad in Retirement

Who hasn't dreamed of spending their retirement years living in an exotic locale far away from the hustle of work and the frequent snowstorms of a New England winter?

More Americans are considering retiring abroad, according to AARP. Some of the top locations when cost and climate are factored in are Belize, Panama, Mexico, Buenos Aires, and Thailand.

Much of Europe may price you out of the market when you compare the costs to remaining stateside. However, a retired friend in the south of Spain assures us that reasonable accommodations can be found—especially with economic turmoil throughout the European Union.

Before you pull up your stakes and sell the ranch, you will need to do some heavy research and soul searching. I would strongly encourage you to spend an extended period of time in the region of your dreams to make sure it is a good fit for you. If you can't live without a Starbucks and a Target on every corner, and your second-language skills are suspect, be prepared for a period of culture shock.

Health care is a major issue for expatriates. Medicare doesn't work outside of our borders, forcing many to purchase additional health insurance coverage or make trips home for their care, which can lead to higher costs and inconvenience.

Other issues to contend with include different forms of government and barriers to those who speak only English.

It's important to find out how your destination country handles taxation of U.S. Social Security benefits and any continuing income you may receive. You must also take into consideration the stability of the local government.

Currency fluctuations will also come into play. Some countries are pegged to the U.S. dollar and others are not. Having several months or more of living expenses in the local currency is not a bad idea since large fluctuations in exchange rates are not uncommon.

Expatriate communities and forums abound. Just be sure to watch out for the real estate marketers who regularly troll these websites and speak at expatriate forums. Some of the complaints that you hear on a regular basis have to do with real estate transactions and developments that have gone badly.

With that caveat in mind, you may want to start by going online and getting involved with some of the online forums for expatriates and people like you who are considering joining their ranks. You can learn a lot from those who have been there and done that.

SPECIAL TOPICS

Raising Financially Savvy Kids

Raising financially independent and savvy children and grandchildren is a goal that every family should place high on the "to do" list. Teaching your children about the value of a buck and about working towards their goals can be a great family activity that helps them develop into financially knowledgeable adults.

Begin when your children learn to count and start filling their piggy banks with their extra change. As they grow older, teach them the basic concepts of value and necessity. A recent Junior Achievement session that I taught for first graders included a course on understanding the difference between needs and desires. Pointing out objects such as food, housing, and electronic games and gadgets led to discussions about their necessity. Best of all, the kids had a great time with the exercise. This can be a great starting point for discussion with your youngsters.

From there, open up a passbook savings account and fund it with a weekly allowance—say $3 to $5 for kids under ten and $10 for teenagers. Deposit some or all of the money providing they follow through on their chores.

Have your children set a goal for a major purchase, such as a bicycle, and enjoy watching them work hard toward reaching their goal. The satisfaction from earning something instead of whining for it can be tremendous. In an era filled with entitlement mindsets, providing healthy incentive-based plans can favorably impact your child's future. Consider offering to pay half the cost of a major item, which provides a lesson about economic incentives and should add motivation to follow through.

As your children grow into young teens, they will become more interested in shopping at the mall for clothes, videogames, electronics, and other items, and this presents a great educational opportunity. You can accompany your child to various stores and point out the comparative values involved. For instance, show them how many shirts they can buy at a discount retailer for the same price they might buy one shirt at a major department store.

Before setting off for the mall, sit down with your child and help him or her draw up a budget for the shopping expedition, then encourage them to stick to that budget in the face of the inevitable temptation to spend more.

The Internet offers a wide variety of sites dedicated to helping educate your budding tycoon. To gain some ideas, visit Junior Achievement (www.ja.org), the National Endowment for Financial Education (www.nefe.org), the Financial Industry Regulatory Authority (www.finra.org), and the JumpStart Coalition for Personal Financial Literacy (www.jumpstart.org).

It's never too early to start teaching your child the value of saving for their future. Even if some of the lessons don't appear to sink in now, you are laying a foundation for understanding that will help your child as he or she grows into an adult and begins to grapple with the difficult choices involved in handling money.

Buying Your Dream Car

Right up there with speaking in public, buying a new car can bring on a cold sweat, even for the most seasoned veterans of the car-buying game. The key to walking into the showroom with confidence lies in proper preparation. Follow these steps when purchasing your dream car:

- **Test-drive several models** that fit your lifestyle, family size, and financial circumstances. Check the reviews of each model in *Consumer Reports*.

- **Go to Edmunds.com** after choosing a model and plug in the car's information, including options such as leather seats or a sunroof. A screen call "TMV" (True Market Value) will give you an approximate idea of what others are paying in our region and will usually include dealer incentives.

- **Look further for incentives** by visiting the national website for the auto company and the websites of area auto dealers. Also, check the auto ads in the newspapers for special prices offered by local dealers.

- **If no incentives are being offered,** ideally you should not pay more than several hundred dollars over invoice for low- to mid-range priced automobiles. You may end up paying more than that for luxury models, especially if they are in high demand.

- **If you have a car to sell or trade in,** use the Edmunds site again and plug in your old car's information to obtain a ballpark figure for its worth. After you receive prices on your new car purchase, ask each competing dealer what they would give you if you traded in the car. Keep in mind the price offered by the dealer will usually be lower than if you sold the car to a private party. You will want to weigh the convenience and cost factors when choosing whether to trade your car in or sell it yourself.

- **If you're financing the car,** check several sources for loan terms and interest rates, including banks, credit unions, and the terms offered by the car company.

- **If you're leasing**, shop several dealers for the best terms available and ask if regular maintenance and service are covered by the lease payment. Compare mileage allowance, penalties for exceeding the limits, and whether or not your town's taxes are included in the payments you make.

Buying a new car should be fun and exciting—not a dreaded chore. Develop the confidence to make it an enjoyable process by taking a positive attitude and doing your homework.

Getting the Right Price for Your Family Business

The largest retirement asset on a business owner's net worth statement is often the family business. When considering an exit strategy, a proper valuation and thorough review of the business, its customer base, and its profitability are in order.

High on the punch list is the need to have a comprehensive, written financial plan in place for yourself. The plan will help you define an objective amount of money that you need to receive for the family business in order to fund the retirement lifestyle you desire. It will clarify how much after-tax money you will need to make on the sale, and will incorporate all of your retirement assets, Social Security benefits, and other income sources. The plan will also address your personal spending and goals in retirement such as travel, hobbies, and interests.

Selling a business can be an unnatural event: Your business and its imperfections will be on display, and your ability to clean up its faults, clarify its mission, and make a solid case for sustained growth upon your departure will drive the purchase price.

- **Start with a credible valuation firm** that knows your industry. When looking for a valuation firm, speak with your CPA, corporate attorney, and other business owners in your industry who have been through this process before. However, keep in mind that once you start talking about valuations and the possibility of a sale, the word can get out. During this process, you would be wise to have nondisclosure agreements signed, but news may still travel. A proper valuation will give you an assessment of your company's strengths and weaknesses and an idea of what prices similar businesses have generated.

- **Smaller businesses may consider a business broker**, but companies with more than $1 million in sales tend to work with merger and acquisition firms. The quality of these firms will run the gamut so do your homework before hiring. Potential buyers will look for reoccurring revenue streams, strong management, an accurate accounting from at least three years of records, and a stable client list. Larger firms may explore the possibility of going public.

- **Once you find a potential buyer the dance begins.** The sales process can take more than a year and can be filled with drama. Having a strong team of advisors in place will give you the best chance of keeping you and the process on track when emotions start to run high. Ideally you will have several suitors for your enterprise. Along the way, your vocabulary will grow to learn what EBITA (Earnings Before Interest, Taxes, and Amortization) means. Offers will often be a multiple of this number, which reflects a company's overall profitability, and will vary, based on the industry and other factors.

Finding the perfect suitor can be a challenge. Ideally you will find a buyer who reflects the values of your organization and your client base. If you plan on staying on for an extended period, you may need an additional "gut check" to make sure the buyer is someone you can actually work with.

Protect Yourself against Identity Theft

A friend of mine had his all-in-one printer/fax machine replaced under warranty recently. When he set up the new printer it automatically printed out the name, Social Security number and address of a local attorney. If you happen to be an identity thief, that's some valuable information.

Apparently the attorney had sent a printer in for repairs, and it ended up becoming the replacement machine for my friend. But neither the attorney nor the retailer had properly "cleansed" the printer before sending it out as a refurbished machine.

Fortunately for the attorney, my friend is not an identity thief. But the story shows how private information is floating about in thousands of new ways in today's digital world, and how difficult it is to control the flow. Identity theft is not always the result of someone rummaging through your trash or selling your credit card information after you make a purchase.

If you fall victim to an identity thief, you may spend hundreds of hours trying to undo the damage to your credit or reputation. In the worst cases, identity theft has led to false arrests.

The Federal Trade Commission suggests taking these steps to reduce the chance of having your identity stolen:

- **Shred financial documents** and paperwork with personal information before discarding.

- **Don't carry your Social Security card** in your wallet or write your Social Security number on a check.

- **Don't give out personal information** on the phone, through the mail, or online unless you know whom you are dealing with.

- **Avoid disclosing personal financial information** when using public wireless connections.

- **Never click on links sent in unsolicited emails.** Instead, type in a web address you know.

- **Use firewalls, anti-spyware, and anti-virus software** to protect your home computer, and keep them up to date.

- **Don't use an obvious password** like your birth date, your mother's maiden name, or the last four digits of your Social Security number.

- **Keep your personal information in a secure place at home**, especially if you have roommates, employ outside help, or have work done in your house.

- **Monitor your financial accounts** and billing statements.

- **Watch for bills that do not arrive as expected**, unexpected account statements, denial of credit for no apparent reason, calls or letters about purchases you did not make, and charges on your financial statements that you don't recognize.

- **Inspect your credit reports**.

- **Place a Fraud Alert on your credit reports, which tells** creditors to follow certain procedures before they open new accounts in your name or change your account.

There are many companies now offering protection against identity theft. Geoff Kanner, a CERTIFIED FINANCIAL PLANNER™ professional in North Haven, suggests the following services to his clients, depending on their situation: LifeLock, Identity Guard, and TrustedID.

As you continue to navigate our increasingly complex digital world, be careful out there!

Charitable Giving Comes in Many Forms

There comes a time in a successful person's life when he or she ponders the difference between being successful and living a life of significance. You see this in the recent pact among some of the nation's entrepreneurial billionaires to give back to society through charitable estate planning—done on their own terms, mind you.

For the rest of us mere mortals, leaving a bequest or making the decision to devote time to a good cause may satisfy our charitable urge. High-end financial planners and estate planning attorneys are often able to help you find the perfect balance in making sure your income needs are being met, that loved ones are well taken care of, and that you are making meaningful contributions to your church, synagogue, community, or favorite charity. Here are some of the different tools you might use:

Charitable gift annuity. This provides a way for you to transfer large amounts of cash or property to a charitable organization in exchange for the charity's promise to make fixed annuity payments to you and/or someone else you name. The annuity rate is based on the age and number of annuitants.

Charitable IRA. Taxpayers who are 70½ or older may transfer up to $100,000 a year from their individual retirement account to a qualified charitable organization, and they don't have to count any of those funds as taxable income. The amount can also be counted as part of your annual required minimum distribution.

Life insurance. You can name your favorite charity as the beneficiary of your life insurance policy, assuming the current beneficiary no longer needs the coverage. The proceeds will qualify for the estate tax charitable deduction.

Charitable bequest. You can leave cash or property to a charity from your estate through either your will or a living trust. The term "bequest" simply refers to something you leave to a person or organization after your death. You can leave a specific amount, sign over a percentage of the overall value of your estate, or stipulate that the charity should receive anything left over after the estate has provided for your family.

Foundation. An increasingly popular alternative is to give to charity through private or public foundations or by organizing your own family foundation. Whichever route you go, the idea is to use or establish a tax-exempt, nonprofit entity designed to distribute grants, either to one charity or to multiple organizations or causes that you name.

This list is not exhaustive, and a financial advisor will look at your overall situation and help you determine which giving tool best suits your needs and goals. The first step, though, is to make the decision to give back.

Weighing the Benefits of Renting versus Owning a Home

As real estate prices fell over the last few years, some Connecticut residents have asked whether they are better off renting or buying a home.

A recent Pew Center Research study shows that eight of every ten adults believe that buying a home is the best investment a person can make. The intensity of that belief has fallen significantly though. Also, Pew noted that 44 percent believe it will take more than three years for their home values to recover from levels reached prior to the recession, and 52 percent believe it will take from six years to more than a decade to reach previous high-water marks.

When Pew researchers asked renters whether they rent out of choice or necessity, only 24 percent said they rent out of choice. Most renters say, given the choice, they would own a home. This isn't surprising since the American Dream has always included dreams of home ownership and the ability to retire in comfort.

Renting does boast certain benefits. You don't have to come up with a substantial down payment, and you can usually send major repair bills to the landlord when the furnace breaks down or the air-conditioner expires. It gives you flexibility as well, since you can leave after your lease expires without the hassle of selling a home in a challenging market.

When you buy a home, you normally have to pay thousands of dollars in upfront closing costs along with a down payment. Other cost factors include property taxes, insurance costs, utility costs, and maintenance and upkeep costs. Houses need to be painted from time to time, for instance. You also usually have to take care of a yard with a house, which adds still more costs.

So from a financial standpoint, it only makes sense to buy a house if you plan to live there for at least several years. You need to live in the house long enough to recoup the closing costs and make the other added costs worth it. If you can do that, then owning a home can pay substantial dividends in the long run since housing prices normally appreciate over time. And, of course, you will enjoy the proud feeling that comes with owning your own home, as well.

Inheritance Poses Challenges for Parent and Child

Who hasn't chuckled upon reading this familiar bumper sticker: "I'm spending my children's inheritance."

In the aftermath of the great recession, the median inheritance for baby boomers is an estimated $64,000, according to the Center for Retirement Research at Boston College.

The center estimates that two-thirds of boomer households will receive an inheritance. The bottom 10 percent will receive around $27,000, and the top 10 percent will receive more than $1 million.

The road to receiving an inheritance brings to mind the pothole-plagued roads driven over by our brave soldiers stationed in the deserts of the Middle East: Detours, mines, and insurgents are stationed along the route.

For the parents of baby boomers, roadblocks to leaving an inheritance abound in the form of life-prolonging medical advancements that increase the need for nursing home stays, inflation at the gas pump and the grocery store, and ever-rising medical costs.

For long-term savers who worked long hours over their lifetimes to accumulate enough assets to leave an inheritance, we suggest getting to know the financial values and spending habits of your beneficiaries. If your loved one is a big spender, a well-placed trust with reasonable restrictions will allow the trustee to maneuver when the beneficiary wishes to make poor financial choices.

Shelby Wilson, an estate planning attorney at Berchem, Moses & Devlin PC in Milford, said more of her clients are facing challenges when it comes to protecting their beneficiaries from outside factors such as divorce, foreclosure, lawsuits, and economic misfortune.

"Well-planned trusts can provide peace of mind for those leaving estates behind, allowing for their loved ones to pay off debt, enjoy additional income, and possibly stretch the monies through succeeding generations," she said.

For baby boomers themselves, we suggest reducing the inheritance assumption in your retirement planning. In fact, you should simply consider any inheritance funds that materialize to be an unexpected blessing.

If you are fortunate enough to come into "sudden money" in the form of an inheritance, take time to consider its best use. We have all heard of the lottery winners and inheritors who blew it all—and then some.

Unless you want to end up as an example of Benjamin Franklin's dictum, "A fool and his money are soon parted," look at your current needs, debts, and goals before deciding how to use your inheritance. For instance, do you need to put aside money for college education of loved ones? That is probably a more sensible choice than buying that cherry-red Corvette you've always dreamed about taking out on the open road.

Discussing the Future with Your Elderly Parents

One of the most challenging but rewarding conversations you can have with your aging parents is about their finances and their planning. Since the topic is considered taboo in some families, you may find out too late that bills haven't been paid or that your parents, who had always assured you that they were fine, are now in need of help.

Unfortunately, many children find out how well their parents have planned only when a crisis hits the home front. You can avoid that by addressing the issues ahead of time.

Here is a list of items that you need to get your arms around for the sake of everyone involved:

- **Wills and living wills.** Do your parents have updated wills and living wills? Beyond that basic step, you also need to make sure it's clear who will have power of attorney to make decisions on their behalf if the need arises.

- **Advisors.** Do you have a list of all your parents' advisors? This could include financial advisors, an attorney, an accountant, insurance agents, religious leaders, counselors, physicians, and other health agents.

- **Assets and investments.** Are your parents' finances set up to last throughout their likely lifetime? You should have a complete list of their bank accounts, investments, insurance policies, property, and other financial interests.

- **Medical insurance.** Do your parents have the proper insurance coverage to pay for medications, health-care bills, and long-term care needs? If not, do they have a plan in place to pay for these needs?

- **Plans for care and beyond.** What are your parents' thoughts and plans when it comes to retirement living and the potential need for assisted living services or end-of-life care? Have they made funeral and burial arrangements in advance?

You may need to tread carefully on these topics depending on your relationship with your parents. One strategy is to ease into the discussion by bringing up your own financial planning, estate plans, or investments. You can share stories about what your friends have dealt with or share an article like this one.

However you approach these subjects, be sure to convey that you care about your parents and want them to enjoy their retirement years without undue worry over financial matters.

With any luck, this conversation will be less awkward than the other talk you may have had with your parents back in your adolescence. Sure is funny how the roles reverse along the way!

How to Find the Right Financial Planner

Choosing the right financial planner can be one of the most important decisions you ever make. After all, the ideal financial advisor is not just someone who will invest your money—they should become a close partner in fulfilling your life's dreams.

There are many reasons to seek out a financial planner: a pending retirement, selling or passing on the family business, leaving an estate with minimal tax impact, a windfall such as an inheritance, reviewing corporate compensation and stock option plans, planning for a marriage or divorce, saving for college, or even handling the loss of a job.

When the need arises, think about what you would do if you needed to find the perfect doctor: You would enlist the help of your social network. A good place to start is with your friends, family, coworkers, and trusted advisors. Ask them if they have a relationship with a financial planner, and if so would they recommend him or her, and why?

Once you compile a list of names, go online to get a feel for each advisor's background and services. One helpful website is www.fpa-net.org, which offers a planner search tool and includes checklists of questions to ask prospective advisors. Also, www.sec.gov and www.finra.org offer information about advisors and brokers including licensing and disciplinary history.

Once you narrow your list, interview several financial planners in order to find the best fit for you and your family. When you visit a planner, here are some questions to ask:

- What are your areas of **specialization**, and what services do you provide?

- What professional **certifications** have you earned? (Look for the CERTIFIED FINANCIAL PLANNER™ certification, since CFP®s are required to have a higher level of financial education and experience and are held to the highest ethical standards.)

- How much investment **experience** do you have, and what licenses do you carry?

- How do you **charge** for your services?

- What is your **approach**? (You need to understand whether a planner believes in a long-term approach to investing or takes an aggressive stance; whether they take the time to get to know your overall situation and understand your life goals or concentrate solely on investing; and whether they have the experience and knowledge to offer broader services such as estate planning.)

A final tip: Beware of any financial advisor who claims the ability to outperform the market. A good advisor will discuss how much risk you are comfortable with, will ask you about your goals and timing, and will talk about ensuring that your investments are properly diversified and regularly rebalanced. If they brag about making a killing, move on to your next advisor interview.

Made in the USA
Charleston, SC
26 February 2013